*Cool*

# MAPS &
# GEOCACHING

*Great Things to Do in the Great Outdoors*

Katherine Hengel

**Checkerboard
Library**

An Imprint of Abdo Publishing
abdopublishing.com

# abdopublishing.com

Published by Abdo Publishing, a division of ABDO,
PO Box 398166, Minneapolis, Minnesota 55439.
Copyright © 2016 by Abdo Consulting Group, Inc.
International copyrights reserved in all countries. No
part of this book may be reproduced in any form without
written permission from the publisher. Checkerboard
Library™ is a trademark and logo of Abdo Publishing.

Printed in the United States of America,
North Mankato, Minnesota
062015
092015

Content Developer: Nancy Tuminelly
Design and Production: Jen Schoeller, Mighty Media, Inc.
Series Editor: Liz Salzmann
Photo Credits: Frankie and Maclean Potts, Jen Schoeller,
Shutterstock

The following manufacturers/names appearing in
this book are trademarks: 3M™ Scotch®, Craft Smart®,
Crayola®, Duck Tape®, Elmer's® Glue-All®, Krylon®
ColorMaster™, Mod Podge®, Rust-oleum® Painter's Touch®,
Scribbles®, Sharpie®

**Library of Congress Cataloging-in-Publication Data**
Hengel, Katherine.
  Cool maps & geocaching : great things to do in the great
outdoors / Katherine Hengel.
    pages cm -- (Cool great outdoors)
  Includes index.
  ISBN 978-1-62403-695-8
1. Geocaching (Game)--Juvenile literature. 2. Global
Positioning System--Juvenile literature. 3. Maps--
Juvenile literature. 4. Orienteering--Juvenile literature.
5. Outdoor recreation--Juvenile literature. I. Title.
  GV1202.G46H46 2016
  796.5--dc23
                      2014045312

## To Adult Helpers:

This is your chance to inspire kids to get outside! As children complete the activities in this book, they'll develop new skills and confidence. They'll even learn to love and appreciate the great outdoors!

Some of the activities in this book will require your help, but encourage kids to do as much as they can on their own. Be there to offer guidance when needed, but mostly be a cheerleader for their creative spirit and natural inspirations!

Before getting started, it helps to review the activities and set some ground rules. Remind kids that cleaning up is mandatory! Adult supervision is always recommended. So is going outside!

## Key Symbols:

In this book you may see these symbols. Here is what they mean:

**HOT STUFF!**
This project requires the use of a stove, oven, or campfire. Always use pot holders when handling hot objects.

**SHARP!**
This project requires the use of a sharp object. Get help.

# CONTENTS

# Find It!

**M**aps are great! They help you find your way to new places. There are many kinds of maps. Some show roads and highways. Others show park trails. There are also maps of bus routes, shopping malls, and more.

We spend most of our lives inside. Take a second to count the hours. You sleep inside. You eat inside. You study inside. That's life in the 21st century.

You've got to get out!

Have you ever used a map? Do you know how? It's not hard to learn. Plus, you can make a homemade compass. You can create and hide your own geocaches! It all happens outside. And it's all good. They don't call it the great outdoors for nothing!

## A NATURAL RECHARGE!

What's so great about the great outdoors? A lot! Being outside exposes us to the sun's natural light. The sun gives us **vitamin** D. Vitamin D keeps our bodies strong! Exposure to sunlight helps regulate our sleeping patterns. The more you are outside, the easier it is to fall asleep!

# EXPLORE YOUR WORLD

*T*hink there's no more world to explore? Think again! You might pass by a park or field every day. But have you ever really explored those places? Do you know what the ground feels like? Or what kind of trees grow there?

Exploration is all about learning more about your **environment**. As you explore, it helps to know where you are! That's why exploration and navigation have always gone hand in hand.

## EVOLUTION *of* NAVIGATION

### SUN AND STARS

How did early explorers know where they were? They used the sun by day and the stars by night!

### MAPS

The earliest maps date back to ancient times. People drew what they saw around them.

### COMPASSES

Written records indicate that people in China began using compasses in the 800s.

### GLOBAL POSITIONING

Global positioning systems (GPS) became popular in the late 1990s.

# GEOCACHING?

Centuries ago, explorers looked for new land. Pirates looked for treasure. What can you look for today? How about a geocache?

A geocache is a container of items that has been hidden. The hider posts the geographic **coordinates** of the geocache online. The coordinates tell geocache hunters the general location of the geocache. Then they are on their own! Geocaching is the art of hiding and finding geocaches.

# GEOCACHING FAQ

**① Do I need a GPS device to geocache?**

Yes and no. The location of a geocache is given in GPS **coordinates**. But some explorers find geocaches using a map, a compass, and their wits!

**② Where do people hide geocaches?**

Anywhere! Geocaches can be in tree branches or under park benches. They can even be hidden in logs or under rocks.

**③ What will I find in a geocache?**

Anything! Coins and small statues are common. There is also usually a **logbook**. It has information about the person who hid the geocache. And it has room for visitors to sign and add information.

**④ Why do people geocache?**

Finding a geocache is exciting. It gets you moving and it gets you outside. It's also a way to meet other geocachers!

# SAFETY FIRST

## in the Great Outdoors

Exploring your world can be a lot of fun. But you need to be prepared. Always know where you are going. Ask for directions. Always be sure you can find your way back.

## Do You Have Permission?

Some of the activities in this book require adult **supervision**. When in doubt, ask for help! More importantly, never go into the great outdoors without an adult. Invite one along for the adventure!

## ARE YOU READY?

☑ **Check the Weather.** Check the forecast before you begin any outdoor adventure!

☑ **Dress Appropriately.** Dress in layers! Be prepared for a **variety** of temperatures.

☑ **Carry Water and Food.** Drinking water keeps you **hydrated**. Snacks give you energy.

☑ **Clean up After Yourself.** Leave things looking at least as good as you found them. Carry your trash and dispose of it properly.

☑ **Bring Emergency Gear.** Carry a whistle, a flashlight, and a first aid kit. Use the whistle if you get lost.

*Now let's get out and enjoy the great outdoors!*

# Materials

Here are some of the things you'll need.

acrylic paint

air-dry clay

aluminum foil

baking sheet

bottle caps

card stock

clear tape

coffee grounds

cork board

craft foam

craft glue

duct tape

flour

glass container

GPS device

magnets

measuring cups
& spoons

mixing bowl

Mod Podge
Dimensional Magic

paintbrush

metal
needle

plastic bag

pot holder

puffy paint

paper

pen

pushpins

ruler

salt

sand

scissors

spray paint

string

twine

US map

vacation pictures

# GET geocaching!

## Get the lowdown on geocaching!

### Materials

GPS device or smartphone with GPS
Geocache Bottle Caps (see pages 18-19)
Secret Cache (see pages 20-21)
Adventure Journal (see pages 28-29)
pen

## Geocaching Near You

There are many clubs and websites for geocachers. Go online to find ones near you. Here are three websites that will get you started.

geocaching.com
opencaching.com
gpsgames.org

## General Guidelines

**1** Follow any instructions provided by the hider.

**2** Geocaches often include things for visitors to take. If you take something, you have to leave something.

**3** Sign the **logbook**.

**4** Do not move or remove a cache.

**5** Keep the secret. Don't show caches you find to people who aren't playing.

### Find a Cache

**1** Visit a geocaching website or join a club! Get geocaching **coordinates** to a site near you.

**2** Enter the coordinates into your GPS device. They should get you within a few feet of the cache. Many caches include hints to help you find them!

**3** Once you find the cache, open it! Many caches are hidden in plastic containers.

**4** Sign the **logbook**. Take out an item. Add your own item in return.

**5** Leave the cache exactly where you found it.

**6** Record your treasure hunt in your Adventure Journal (see pages 28 to 29). What was difficult? What was fun?

## Hide a Cache

1 Put together a Secret Cache (see pages 20 to 21).

2 Find a good spot to hide your Secret Cache. Make sure not to hide it in a **dangerous** place. Ask **permission** of the property owner before hiding the cache.

3 Use your GPS device to find the **coordinates** of your Secret Cache. Write them down.

4 Visit a geocaching website! Post the GPS coordinates. Add some hints for people looking for your cache.

5 Check on your cache every once in a while. See who has visited!

# GEOCACHE
# bottle caps

**Make a calling card to leave when you're geocaching!**

## Materials

newspaper
spray paint
bottle cap
patterned paper
ruler
scissors
craft glue
Mod Podge Dimensional Magic
self-adhesive magnet

1 Cover your work surface with newspaper. Spray paint the bottle cap. Use several light coats so the paint doesn't run. Let it dry completely after each coat.

2 Cut a 1-inch (2.5 cm) circle out of patterned paper.

3 Glue the circle inside the bottle cap. Cover it with a thick layer Mod Podge Dimensional Magic. It will be clear when it's dry.

4 Peel the **backing** off the magnet. Stick the magnet to the back of the cap.

**TIP**

Make a bunch of bottle caps! You can put one in each geocache you find.

# SECRET cache

**Make a rock to disguise your cache!**

## Materials

baking sheet
aluminum foil
measuring cups
mixing bowl
mixing spoon
1 cup coffee grounds
1 cup sand
1 cup salt
1 cup flour
1 cup water
newspaper
8-ounce glass container
pot holders

**HOT!**

1 **Preheat** the oven to 250 degrees. Cover the baking sheet with aluminum foil.

2 Put the coffee grounds, sand, salt, and flour in a mixing bowl. Stir the ingredients together. Slowly add the water until the mixture sticks together.

3 Cover your work surface with newspaper. Mold the dough around the outside of the glass container.

4 Place the molded dough on the baking sheet. Bake for 25 minutes. Take it out. Turn the dough over. Bake for 10 more minutes. Take it out and let it cool.

5 Take out the glass container. This is your fake rock. You can hide your geocache beneath it.

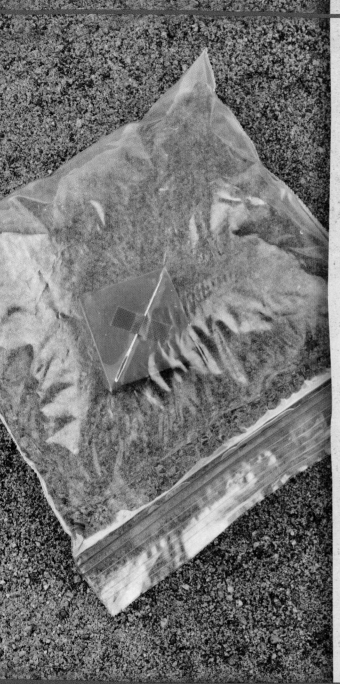

# plastic bag
# COMPASS

**Explore the unknown with a homemade compass!**

## *Materials*

magnet or magnetizer
large metal needle
craft foam
ruler
scissors
duct tape
water
plastic bag

SHARP!

1. Slide the magnet along the needle from the eye to the point. Repeat for 2 to 3 minutes. Or stick the pointed end of the needle in a magnetizer for 3 minutes.

2. Cut a 1-inch (2.5 cm) square out of craft foam.

3. Duct tape the middle of the needle to the center of the foam square.

4. Fill the plastic bag three-quarters full of water. Drop the foam square in with the needle on top. Close the bag. Make sure it still has some air in it. Lay the bag on its side. The magnetized end of the needle will point north.

**TIP**

Leave the needle in a magnetizer for a full day. It will work as a compass for up to two weeks!

# CUBE
## walkers

Make every walk
an adventure!

*Materials*

newspaper
air-dry clay
ruler
black & white acrylic paint
paintbrushes

1 Cover your work surface with newspaper. Form the clay into a cube. Make it 2 inches (5 cm) on each side. Let it dry for 24 hours.

2 Paint the cube white. Let the paint dry. Add another coat if necessary.

3 Paint an arrow on each side of the cube. Let the paint dry.

4 Go on a hike. Roll the cube to decide which way to go.

On the photos:

North Woods, MN  June 20, 2015
Maria, Kelly, Henry, & Mike

Tampa, Florida  April 15,
Josh, Pam, Chris, Aaron

# marvelous
# MAP

## Make a map of your travels!

### Materials

US map
clear tape
large corkboard
vacation pictures
pushpins
scissors
card stock
pen
string

*1* Tape the map to the corkboard.

*2* Pin your vacation pictures around the outside of the map.

*3* Cut the card stock into strips. Use the strips to make a label for each picture. Include the date and location. Add the names of the people in the picture. Tape the labels by their pictures.

*4* Tie the string to one of the pins holding a picture. Put a pin on the map where the picture was taken. Tie the other end of the string to the pin on the map. Cut off the extra string.

*5* Repeat step 4 with the rest of the pictures.

*6* Add more pictures as you go to different places.

**If you've been to other countries, use a world map. Or use a map of your state or city.**

# adventure JOURNAL

**Make a book to write about your trips!**

## Materials

card stock
ruler
scissors
paper
twine
puffy paint

1. Cut a rectangle out of card stock. Make it 3 by 12 inches (7.5 by 30 cm). Cut 10 sheets of paper the same size.

2. Lay the paper on top of the card stock. Fold everything in half crosswise. Press firmly to crease the card stock and paper. Then unfold it.

3. Punch two holes along the fold. Go through the paper and card stock. Thread the twine through the holes. Tie the ends together. Cut off the extra twine.

4. Use puffy paint to decorate the front cover.

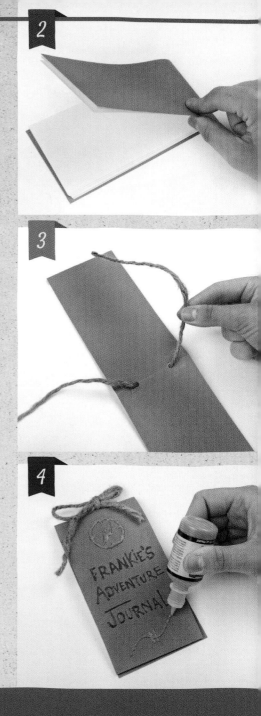

# How Great Is the GREAT OUTDOORS?

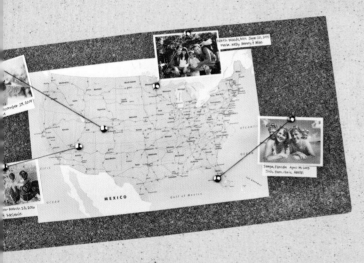

id you enjoy the map and geocaching activities in this book? Did any of them inspire you to do more things in the great outdoors?

There is so much to love about being outside. These activities are just the beginning! Check out the other books in this series. You just might start spending more time outside than inside!

# GLOSSARY

**backing** – the paper that covers the sticky side of something, such as a stamp or sticker.

**coordinate** – one of two numbers used to locate a point on a plane.

**dangerous** – able or likely to cause harm or injury.

**environment** – nature and everything in it, such as the land, sea, and air.

**hydrated** – having enough water or moisture.

**logbook** – a book for keeping records, such as a journal or a diary.

**permission** – when a person in charge says it's okay to do something.

**preheat** – to heat an oven to a certain temperature before putting in the food.

**supervision** – the act of watching over or directing others.

**variety** – different types of one thing.

**vitamin** – a substance needed for good health, found naturally in plants and meats.

## Websites

To learn more about Cool Great Outdoors, visit **booklinks.abdopublishing.com**. These links are routinely monitored and updated to provide the most current information available.

# Index